WAY-OUT IDEAS

FOR YOUTH GROUPS

WAY-OUT IDEAS FOR YOUTH GROUPS

Compiled by
MIKE YACONELLI and WAYNE RICE

ZONDERVAN
PUBLISHING HOUSE
OF THE ZONDERVAN CORPORATION | GRAND RAPIDS, MICHIGAN 49506

CONTENTS

INTRODUCTION

Congratulations! You have just purchased a book that is absolutely worthless . . . unless you read this chapter carefully.

Way Out Ideas for Youth Groups is a compilation of the best youth programming ideas in use today. Every idea in this book has been used successfully in youth programs all over the country. But possessing a book of good ideas isn't enough. We have found that certain ingredients must be present for an idea to be effective. So before you run out and use the ideas in this book, take time to find out **how** to use them.

THE INGREDIENT OF HUMOR

Many church groups voice opposition to the use of humor in youth programs. We have listed five of the most common reasons given:

1. Humor Can Only Be Done Well by Certain Personalities

What makes a person funny **is** his personality. The important thing is to determine what in **your** personality makes people laugh. All of us can be humorous as long as we be ourselves and do not try to compete with or imitate others.

2. Our Group Doesn't Respond to Humor

There are many reasons a group doesn't respond to humor. First of all, they may not have had anything to laugh at. Or the room may discourage laughter because it's too formal or too large. The best setting for kids is an informal, small room where they can relax.

It may be that your young people are afraid to laugh because they feel that God and laughter don't go together. Whatever the reasons, let's understand that all groups respond to humor if you give them a chance.

3. Humor Is Not Appropriate

Many feel that humor does not fit in a church-related service. They feel it is disrespectful to God and the church. Humor does not always have to be a distraction; it can also enhance a program, as you will see in this book.

4. Humor Is Shallow

Many groups have dismissed any humorous activities as shallow and unnecessary. They say their group feels a need to discuss basic issues rather than waste time with fun and games. We're not suggesting that humor is **necessary**, we only say that used in a balanced program, it is anything but shallow.

5. Humor Is Different in Our Area

Although it is true that certain areas have localized humor, it is equally true that if something is funny most everyone will laugh. The point is, the ideas in this book will work anywhere in this country. They already have.

THE INGREDIENT OF TIMING

The success of every crowd breaker, skit, game or activity depends upon its timing. Anytime young people are involved in a program, it is vital to keep the program moving with no time lags. Here are some helpful hints about timing:

1. Always have all props and equipment readily accessible. There should be no vocal pause while you are hunting or reaching for the necessary equipment.

2. Set time limits for each event. Time limits should be judged by the audience response, not by the hand of the watch. In other words, if the event was to be thirty seconds and the audience is bored, end it early. Call time whenever an activity is dragging or not going over.

3. Know what you're going to do before you begin. Never read off a script, if possible.

4. Always check out the location of the event first. Decide the best seating

arrangement ahead of time. Make sure there is plenty of room for movement without breaking anything.

5. Set up film or recording equipment ahead of time and double check to make sure you have plenty of cord and an available electrical outlet.
6. Use applause and cheering to fill in dead spots. Encourage a general audience response to any activity being performed.
7. Divide group into teams that cheer for contestants or participants. Further motivation can be encouraged by threatening a penalty to the least enthusiastic team.
8. You are not a slave to a schedule or activity. If something is not going over, stop it. If you have chosen three contestants and two have not been effective, cancel the third.
9. Always build to the punch line or ending, but never drag it out. Leave the audience laughing and wanting more. Don't drain them until they cannot laugh any longer.
10. Be selective with both the leader and participants. Don't allow someone to ruin a skit or crowd breaker because he is shy, too slow, etc.
11. Always have an alternative. Be prepared in case something goes wrong with the planned activity and have an alternate plan ready and waiting.
12. Insure success by "fixing" certain stunts. Inform the victim privately of his fate and ask him to go along.
13. Don't rely on kids to run the activities in this book. These are generally activities for them to participate in under leader direction.

THE AUDIENCE INGREDIENT

Every audience is different. As a leader, you must use the audience in the most effective way:

1. Use key people, well-known to the group. If well-known people are participating, the activity will be considered in a more favorable light.
2. Have the group choose the contestants. (Be careful that their choice isn't someone they want to ridicule.)
3. Use leaders or popular adults in the activities. Let the group know the leaders aren't immune from the activities.
4. Take advantage of a loudmouth or attention-getter. Involve him in an activity in which he is the victim and let the audience enjoyment put him in his place.

This book contains the best crowd breakers, stunts, games, skits, and creative communication ideas in use today. Their effectiveness with your group depends on you. We hope you recognize that the contents of this book are meant to be a **supplement** to your youth program. This book was written as a source of workable materials that will help you attract and interest kids in what you have to say. We are not suggesting that your youth programs should be fun times or skit nights. We have assumed that you have a message to give to young people. Hopefully, you have a solid program and philosophy in which you've recognized your responsibility and opportunity to share the Gospel of Jesus Christ with your young people. **Way Out Ideas for Youth Groups** was never meant to be a substitute for the message of Christ. It is to be used, rather, as a means of communication that will reach an otherwise unreachable young person with the hope of salvation and redemption.

CROWD BREAKERS AND SKITS

As far as programming is concerned, the success of any type of meeting is usually determined by what takes place in the first ten minutes. It is during this time that people (young people, especially) get turned on or off to the program and those connected with it. For example, when you turn on a T.V. program, you probably judge the entire show on the first few minutes. If it starts out bad, you simply change channels or turn the T.V. off. But in a youth meeting, kids will usually just turn their brains off.

The Crowd Breakers in this book are designed to be used primarily as "program starters." When properly used, they become effective tools for winning the attention of any group of young people in almost any situation. Crowd Breakers are fun activities which call everyone in the group in either indirect (observance) or direct (involvement) participation, and inevitably result in a lot of laughs and a well-balanced program.

One type of Crowd Breaker is the "Group Participation Activity" in which the entire audience involves actively in an unskilled, non-competitive game. The "Flypaper Pass" and the "Question and Answer Game" are good examples of this. Both are great games that can be played by the group without leaving their seats and in both cases, everyone is involved. This kind of activity helps each person feel more like an important part of the meeting itself.

Another type of Crowd Breaker is the "Fall Guy Stunt." Examples are the "Alum Ice Cream Eat" and "Bucket Roulette" in which the group watches one of its members receive a crazy consequence of some kind. This provides a lot of laughs and is excellent for warming up an otherwise cold audience. It is often advised to "fix" these stunts so that a "bomb" is avoided. The "fall guy" is clued in ahead of time that he is going to get it, and the result is a successful Crowd Breaker. "Fixing" is, of course, dependent on individual circumstances and should not be done in every case.

A third type of Crowd Breaker is the "Competition Stunt." The audience watches a contest between two or more people in much the same way as they would observe a football or baseball game. The difference is that the competition is on a much smaller scale and that it is unusual and fun to watch. The "Rubberband Relay" is a good competition stunt that has its appeal in watching guys (or girls) distort their faces trying to move a rubber band from their nose to their chin. Appropriate crazy prizes and penalties should always be on hand to award the winners and the losers.

Regardless of the "type," the primary purpose of a Crowd Breaker is to make the audience laugh. Laughter is a healthy indication that the crowd is enjoying what is going on and is ready for more.

GAMES AND SPECIAL EVENTS

The key to a successful youth activity such as a social, party, camp, retreat or all day outing is often in the types of games used. When most young people think of "games," they immediately have visions of ping-pong, volleyball or "drop the hanky," which usually fail to turn on the average twentieth-century student.

Games used with today's youth, particularly in a church situation, require most, if not all, of the following characteristics. First, they should be unlike any other game that is typically played by the group at school, home or anywhere else. Kids will then look forward to these games, because they are so unusual and the games will be identified with the program. Whenever the young person remembers the great time he had playing a particularly unusual game, he will also remember the activity, special event, or the youth group.

Good games should also be "unskilled." Many kids feel inferior because they are not athletic or always "come in last," so they refuse to participate in games such as softball or volleyball. However, games like "Mad-Ads" or the "Excedrin Wamp" require no skill or athletic ability whatsoever and everyone is on equal terms.

Another essential ingredient of a successful game is humor. Games should not only be fun to participate in, but they should be inherently funny. For example, the whole idea behind games like the "Toilet Paper Relay" or "Gorilla-Man-Gun" is that they are totally ridiculous. Although competition is involved, it is not taken seriously, and the game is played just for the fun of it.

The purpose of a game is for total involvement and enjoyment by everyone. If at any time a game is dragging or not going over, it should be immediately stopped and another game or event begun. Games should not be played just for the sake of playing a game.

CREATIVE COMMUNICATION

Communication as it relates to teaching is not indoctrination. It is a two-way exchange of ideas which results in discovery. This discovery can be accomplished in many different ways and a few of those ways are included in this compilation of "way out ideas."

Discussions are primary sources of discovery and involvement. Discussion is most effective when stimulated by a relevant news or magazine article, story, survey or film presented by the discussion leader prior to the actual discussion. A good example of this is the "Island Affair," in which a hypothetical story is related to the group which demands a response. It is almost impossible to just "let it lie." Discussion is inevitable.

Another approach to discussion is "Groupers." These "written discussions" are especially good with youth groups that don't like to talk much or they are excellent as a warm-up prior to discussion.

It is important to understand that the biggest hindrance to open and honest communication in the church is often the lack of freedom for young people to say that which may not fit within the confines of "correct" theology. The atmosphere of discussion must be one of complete freedom to express that which one believes, regardless of its adherence to what others believe. Therefore, the leader should only be concerning himself with keeping order rather than guiding the group to the "correct" answers. When the discussion period is over, it is then appropriate for the leader to express his thoughts and opinions, but not in the form of preaching or putting down the opinions expressed by the group. When this is done, young people are more likely to arrive at healthy, lasting discoveries that will result in solid Christian growth.

1. CROWD BREAKERS

1. CROWD BREAKERS

ALUM ICE CREAM EAT

Pick two girls and two guys. Send them out of the room for a minute and explain to audience the sneaky surprise. Bring contestants back. Girls compete first. Put a bib on each of them and give them each a bowl of ice cream. The object is to eat the most within the one minute time limit using only their mouth. The boys then do the same thing. The only difference is that buried in both boys' ice cream is a large amount of alum.

APPLE PARING CONTEST

Have a race to see who can peel the longest continuous strip of peel from an apple.

BABY PICTURE GUESS

Have five or six kids bring their baby pictures to the meeting. Hold them up and have the rest of the group try to guess who they are. Award prizes to anyone who gets them all right.

BALLOON POP

Choose three boys or girls and give each one a balloon. First one to blow balloon until it pops wins. Losers get penalty.

BANDAGED HAND

Let the group know that the following announcement is quite serious and there must be absolute attention. Give the following speech: "I am sorry that I have to put a damper on the meeting tonight, but a few minutes ago, one of our girls came to me really upset. She was sitting down outside and some guy (and you know who you are) came up to her and tried to kiss her. He was trying to be smart, I guess, but the girl didn't think it was very funny, and neither do I. Apparently, he didn't take the hint when she asked him to leave and he reached down and tried to kiss her. The girl got scared, and reacted by stabbing him in the hand with a ball-point pen that she was holding. Now this girl is very upset, and I want to see that guy right after the meeting tonight, and I want you to know that we just do not tolerate that sort of thing around here."

After the speech is over, the person who gave the announcement takes his hand out of his pocket, revealing a hand wrapped with gauze and blood stains all over it.

BIGGER AND BETTER HUNT

Choose two couples and give each an item. They are to go out in the neighborhood and trade it for something better. They might start with an old inner-tube, street marker, broken vase or something like that. Give them fifteen minutes to go out into the neighborhood and trade up for something better that can be kept. Audience judges which one secured the best. The losers get the penalty.

BUCKET ROULETTE

Show audience three pails containing rice, water, and confetti. Bring three contestants out, one at a time, and have them choose one pail to be dumped on them. Be sure to dress contestants in grubbies so their good clothes will not be damaged.

CHIKI-CHIKI

Contestants line up in a straight line with leader at the front of the line. The five boy contestants are to do exactly what the leader does because it is a coordination and creativity test to see (1) how well they can follow the director, and (2) how well they can improvise on what he does. Each boy does what the leader did in sequence. (The leader has a container of lipstick

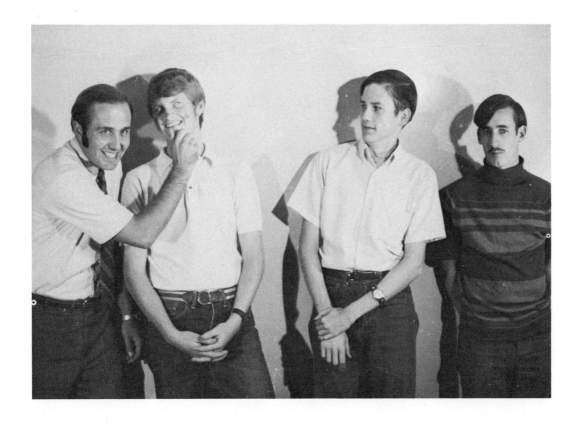

behind him and every time he gives the following instructions he is putting lipstick on the person next to him with his fingers.) Each instruction names a part of the face: cheeky-cheeky, nosey-nosey, chinnie-chinnie, etc. The leader follows each instruction with a circular movement of his hand toward the part of the face mentioned and grabs that part. The leader then pulls out a little pocket mirror, puts it in front of him and says, "mirrey-mirrey," and then gives it to the boy next to him who suddenly sees himself with lipstick all over him.

CHOO-CHOO TO HAWAII

Send a few guys out of the room and bring them in one at a time for this stunt. You have a choo-choo train (made up of boys and girls holding onto each other's waists and moving around the room going ch-ch-ch-ch-ch, etc.), and it is the first choo-choo to Hawaii. You bring in a guy, and ask him to be the caboose. He is instructed to just hang on and do what everyone else does. So the train goes around the room and the guy in front stops the train and says, "Welcome to Hawaii" and puts a Hawaiian lei on the neck of the girl behind him, and gives her a kiss on the cheek. The girl says "Welcome to Hawaii" to the guy behind her, and gives the lei, and kisses the guy on the cheek, and so on, down to the final girl, who takes the lei, puts it around the neck of the last guy (who was brought in), welcomes him to Hawaii, and then slaps him hard on the cheek. The look on his face is priceless, as he was also expecting a kiss.

COMBINED GIRL WEIGHT GUESS

Choose three boys and send them out of the room. Ask the girls (three) for their weights. Add them, and tell audience total. Then bring the guys back into the room, and ask them to guess the total weight of the three girls. Each one guesses, and the one who is closest to the total wins prize; losers get a penalty.

COMPATIBILITY TEST

This crowd-breaker is designed after TV's Newlywed Game. Three couples are chosen, and the three boys leave the room while a set of questions about the boy friends are asked of each of the three girls. Questions such as, "Did he kiss you on your first date?" or "Where did you go on your first date?"

Boys are then brought back into the room and asked the same questions and must answer correctly (same as the girl) or receive penalty such as the "electric chair." Other good questions are: "Would you consider your boyfriend tight, average, or generous when it comes to spending money?" or "Is your boy friend a bad, fair, or good driver?"

CO-ORDINATION CLAP

You cross your hands in a vertical (up and down) manner. The group is instructed to clap once every time your hands cross. The idea is to fake everyone out by almost crossing your hands, etc. Award a penalty of some kind to whoever goofs it. One idea is to keep it up to see who can go the longest without making a mistake.

EAT BANANA — DRINK 7-UP

Pull three boys out of audience who race to see who can peel and eat a banana, then drink a bottle of 7-Up the fastest. The results are hilarious. Loser gets a penalty.

ESKINOSE

Divide group into two teams, alternating by sex. First person has lipstick smear on his nose. Winning team is the one who can pass the lipstick the farthest in thirty seconds by Eskimo kissing (rubbing noses). Winners get Eskimo Pies.

FLYPAPER PASS

Pass a piece of flypaper around from person to person with one hand. Whoever is caught with it in his hand at the end of the period of time gets penalty.

FOOT PAINTING

Choose a group of boys (number of boys should be one half the number of letters in the name of your group, church, organization, etc.). They all sit down in a line facing audience. You paint the letters in the name of your group on the bottom of their feet (jumbled up) with a felt marker or poster paint. At a signal, they are to try and get the letters unscrambled and in order (readable) without any of them getting up or moving from their positions.

FUNNEL TRICK

Place a funnel in a boy's pants (in front). Have him tip his head back, then place a nickel on his forehead. The object is for him to drop the nickel into the funnel three times in succession. The third time pour a cup of water into the funnel while his head is tipped back.

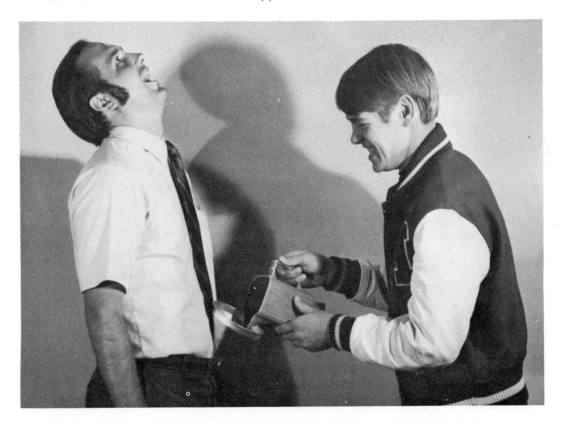

ICE CREAM SUNDAE

Have two or three of your key kids build the "world's largest ice cream sundae" in front of the audience. Use plenty of ice cream, chopped nuts, syrups, cherries, and whipped cream. Build it in a punch bowl or a washtub and afterward pass out paper plates and spoons and let everyone dig in! If you advertise this ahead of time, a good name is an "Ice Cream Scream."

JELLO RACKET

On a warm day, pass a piece of Jello around your group on a tennis racket. Person on whom it falls gets a penalty.

JUNK AUCTION

As a great fun activity and also a great money raiser for your group, collect a lot of interesting "junk" that you think kids might really go for, and auction it off. You'll be surprised at what kids will buy for unbelievable amounts of money. Be creative in your auctioneering, and make funny routines to "sell" your items to your crowd. This works best with a large group. When the bidding is good, the results are hilarious.

KLEENEX BLOW

Have audience divide into groups of ten and have each one form a circle. Give each group a kleenex. Without touching kleenex each group attempts to keep kleenex in the air the longest by blowing. Best time wins.

MARBLE FISH

Fill two pans full of crushed ice and have two guys try to fish out ten marbles placed in the bottom of the pan with their bare toes.

OBSTACLE COURSE

Blindfold a person and have him walk through an obstacle course of chairs, lamps, etc. Let him see the obstacles, blindfold him, then remove all the obstacles.

PEOPLE BINGO

Randomly select people's names to fill in each square on playing boxes below (one name to a square). The best way to do this is to give every kid a playing card like the one illustrated below that is blank, then each kid just looks around the room and puts somebody's name in every square. Then, from a hat, randomly pull kids' names and if a player has that one's name on his card, he marks an "X" through that name. The first person who has a row of "X's" either horizontally, vertically, or diagonally, wins.

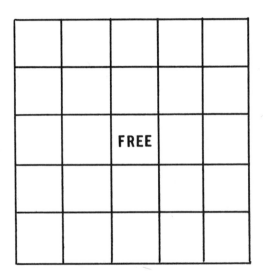

PEOPLE ORGAN

Choose six to eight kids to become a people organ. Have them form a line facing the audience and announce that the organ will "play" a song like "Three Blind Mice." Leader taps person on the head and they are to respond with the appropriate note. This is funniest when you use big husky guys who can't sing.

PING PONG FLOUR BLOW

Have two boys compete to see who can blow a ping pong ball out of a round bowl in the fastest time. Each tries and is timed. Then, to make it even harder, they are to try it blindfolded. The first boy does and is timed. Then the second boy tries. But just before he blows, dump a cup of flour in the bowl.

PLATE HYPNOTISM

Explain to audience that you have had some experience (in college) with hypnotism. Ask for volunteers, "Who will try hard to be hypnotized?" Give them a plate full of magic hypnotic power which they hold in front of them with one hand and you do the same. Then the volunteer does everything you do while looking you straight in the eyes. You rub finger in top of plate

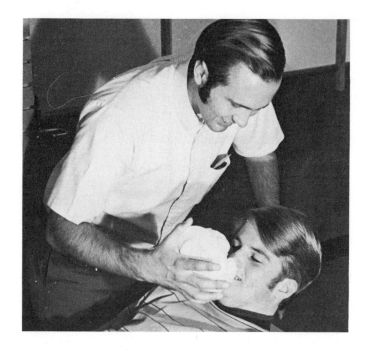

and rub between eyes over and over. Then rub edges and finally the bottom of the plate and rub between eyes. You have charred the bottom of the volunteer's plate with a match, so he rubs black soot on his eyes, unaware of what is going on. Work out a good solid routine for this and it is guaranteed to be a winner.

PSYCHOLOGICAL SIT-UPS

Leader explains that it is possible to prevent someone from sitting up by using certain mental block techniques. He explains that he has become proficient in this technique and asks for volunteers. Three boy volunteers are chosen with two sent out of the room. Each contestant will be asked to do one sit-up to prove they can do one. They are then to lie down on a table with eyes shut and hands flat. They are instructed to keep their eyes shut for the entire exercise or the psychological barrier will be broken. They are then to concentrate on sitting up. From the moment the leader signals the audience to begin chanting, "You can't sit up," they are to concentrate on sitting up. When the leader abruptly cuts the chanting off, the contestants are to sit up immediately. However, while the audience is chanting the leader has filled a pie plate full of shaving cream and when the contestant does sit up he is met with a pie plate full. Each contestant is cleaned up quickly and asked to sit down while the others are brought in one by one.

QUESTION AND ANSWER GAME

Hand out plain cards and pencils to everyone in group. Divide into two teams. Everyone on team 1 will write a question beginning with "how" such as "How do you peel a prune?" Everyone on the other team will write an answer beginning with "by" such as "By using pinking shears." Collect cards, keeping them in two groups, and then read first a question and then an answer. Random reading will produce hilarious results.

QUICK-DRAW CONTEST

Place an easel with a drawing pad on it at the front of the room. Choose two couples, and send them out of the room. The guy stands at the easel with a felt tip pen and the girl faces the audience and is given an object, such as a can opener, a light bulb, a screwdriver, etc. (The guy should not see what the object is.) The girl then tries to describe the object to the boy and the boy tries to draw it from her description, and guess what the object is. The girl cannot use words that would give away what the object is, but must merely describe the shape of it, such as "Draw a straight line about three inches long, and then curve it slightly to the right. . . ." With younger kids, allow the girl to watch the boy as he draws, and give him instructions, correcting, etc. Time the first couple and then bring the second couple in and they do the same thing with the same object. Don't make the object **too** hard.

REVOLVING STORY

Begin at one side of room or in a circle. The first person begins to make up a fairy tale of some kind. He continues for ten seconds and at a signal the next person in line adds to the story for ten seconds and so on down the line. The results are usually quite funny.

RUBBER BAND RELAY

Use three guys in this "face coordination" test. Place a rubber band around each guy's head with it crossing over the tip of his nose. The idea then, is to maneuver the rubber band from the nose down to the neck without using hands. Any facial contortion he can think of is legal.

SKYDIVING LESSON

Three boys are chosen to learn how to skydive. One at a time, each boy is brought into the room and asked to stand on a sturdy 2 x 4 plank, which is lifted up by two strong boys. He uses the leader's head as a brace, so he won't fall. The board is lifted up about three feet, then the contestant is asked to jump into a small circle for five points. The board is lifted higher, and he jumps again for ten points. The last time, for twenty points, he must jump blindfolded. The strong boys, however, only lift the board two or three inches, and the leader stoops down real low, giving the blindfolded contestant the feeling that he is high. He jumps, but usually he falls flat on his face.

STABBING DUEL

Have two boys tie left wrists together. Each takes a banana in his right hand. The object is to one-handedly peel the banana and stab the other boy in the face. The first to do so is the winner.

THE SIT DOWN GAME

Instructions:

1. Ask the entire audience to stand.
2. Instruct them to sit down when the "if" characteristic applies to them and remain seated.
3. Encourage them to be as honest as possible.
4. If you have trouble because most are not sitting down, then give some general characteristic, such as:
   a. Sit down if you are under 15 (over 18, etc.).
   b. Sit down if you have on white socks.
   c. Sit down if you are in love.

SIT DOWN GAME NUMBER ONE

SIT DOWN IF:

You didn't use deodorant today
You have worn the same socks for two days
You sing in the shower
You drive a Volkswagen
Your belly-button is an outie
You kiss with your eyes open
You went to the drive-in this weekend but didn't see the movie
You dated a loser this past weekend
You are a boy and use hairspray
You haven't taken a bath in a week
You kiss sloppy
You have a pimple on your nose

You didn't brush your teeth today
You didn't use any mouthwash today
You are a girl and haven't shaved your legs today
You are a guy and **did** shave your legs today
You are ugly

SIT DOWN GAME NUMBER TWO

SIT DOWN IF:

Your nose is crooked
You read this month's issue of **Playboy**
You believe in necking on the first date
You believe in necking before the first date
You are mad at your girlfriend or boyfriend now
You still suck your thumb
Your socks don't match
You have a bottle opener in your purse
You are ticklish
You wear "baby doll" pajamas
You have dandruff
The person in front of you has dandruff
You walk funny
Your nylon has a run in it
You weigh over 200 pounds
Your nose is running and you don't have a handkerchief
You are going steady, but wish you weren't
You are good looking, but not conceited

SIT DOWN GAME NUMBER THREE

SIT DOWN IF:

You have ever "two-timed" your girlfriend or boyfriend
You have ever eaten snail
You are cross-eyed
Your mother dresses you

You use Ban
You have never been kissed
The person in front of you smells
You have a hole in your sock
You got a traffic ticket recently
You are on a diet
You aren't on a diet but should be
You aren't on a diet, but the person next to you should be
You have ever stolen a street marker
You have a false tooth
You are passionate
You are really good looking
Stand up if the person next to you just sat down and was **wrong**

STANDING BROAD GRIN

Guys or girls have contest to see who can "grin" the widest grin. Use a ruler to measure the winner.

THE ART CLASS

Explain that you are an artist in your spare time and that you are going to paint a "human painting" right before the eyes of the audience. The scene will be in the forest, and you will use people instead of paint. Have someone come up and be the "babbling brook" by standing up front going "babble babble babble . . ." over and over. Next have someone come up and be the rustling trees. He stands next to the babbling brook and goes "rustle rustle rustle . . ." etc. Do the same thing with the "whistling grass" and the "howling wind," and then ask for someone to come up and be the picture frame. The frame runs around the other guys who are babbling, rustling, whistling, howling, etc., and he continues to run around them. While they are all doing their part, you say, "And now, ladies and gentlemen, there you have it. The babbling brook, the rustling trees, the whistling grass, the howling wind, and the **running sap!**"

THE LEGEND OF THE HONEY BEE

Announce to the audience that one of the educational features of your group is to explain frankly "the birds and the bees." But because of lack of time, you will only be able to explain the "bees part" at this time. You choose a volunteer from the audience, and you have him sit in a chair at the front of the room facing the audience. You explain to him that he is the queen bee, the audience is the flower garden, and you are the worker bee. You will go out into the flowers and collect one load of pollen, bring it back, and will say the little bee phrase, "Whompf!" to the queen bee. The queen bee must say it back, which means that the worker bee can go out and collect another load. (Have him try it—audience applauds.) You then bring back a second load of pollen and with your wings fluttering say, "Whompf! Whompf!" The queen bee says it back, and you go out for a third load. This time when you

come back, you have so much pollen that you can't even speak, and so the queen bee must say, "Buzz, Buzz, little bee. Give it all to me!" (On your third load, you go out into the audience and secretly get a mouthful of water. When the queen bee says "Buzz, Buzz, etc." you spray water all over him.)

THE SHOE STRETCH

Get two old pair of men's shoes, take out strings, punch hole in back of each one and tie a four-foot piece of elastic to each. Place shoes on opposite sides of room and tie other ends of the elastic to legs of chair. The object now is for the two people to get into the shoes—one in each pair and walk toward each other. Have someone sitting in the chairs to weight them, and have them spaced so the elastic becomes taut just as the two meet each other. The object is, with the shoes stretching the elastic, to exchange shoes in the fastest time possible and return to the other chair. Several rules:

1. Once one's foot is taken out of shoe, it cannot touch the floor.
2. If shoe snaps back to chair, person must hop back and get it.
3. Hands cannot be used to exchange shoes—you'll need your hands to hold each other up.

THE SUBMARINE RIDE

A volunteer lies flat on a table with a person at each arm and each leg. The legs are the left and right rudders. The arms are Torpedo One and Tor-

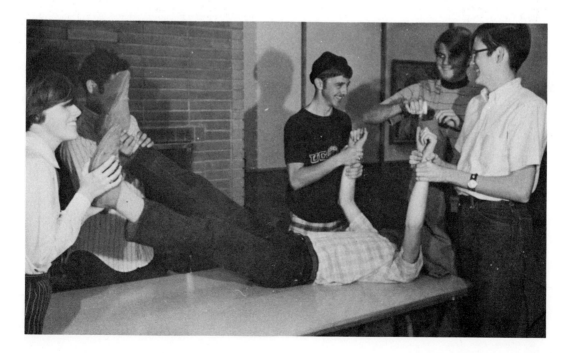

pedo Two. A jacket is put over the volunteer's head with one sleeve directly on his nose. This is the periscope. The captain (you or the leader) yells "Left Rudder!" (person on left leg raises leg). "Right Rudder!" (raise right leg). "Torpedo One! Torpedo Two!" (raise arms). "Up Periscope!" (sleeve is lifted straight up). "Dive! Dive!" (you pour water down sleeve and into the volunteer's face).

THREAD THE NEEDLE

Call three guys up to see who can thread a needle with one eye closed in the fastest time. Give the first guy the needle and thread, appoint a time-keeper, and to assure that he will only use one eye, you put your hand over one of his eyes. Give each guy two tries, using one eye and then the other. On the last guy, smear some lipstick or soot on your hand, and smear it all over the last guy's eyes when you put your hand over his eyes. (Use a large needle or this will take too long.)

WHAT-ER SURPRISE!

This is a trick that you play on the entire audience. You need one helper. You announce that you have a bucket of magic potion, or something of that nature, that will change whoever drinks it in some way. (You can make up your own routine for this.) Have a volunteer come up to try the magic potion (clued in ahead of time). Your bucket is brought into the room, and the audience cannot see inside it, but it is really a bucket of confetti or rice, with a dipper sticking out of the bucket with a little water in it. (The outside of the dipper must be dry so that no confetti or rice will stick to it.) You take the dipper out and pour the water into a glass for the volunteer to drink. He drinks it, screams, and grabs the bucket and throws its contents all over the group.

2. GAMES

2. G A M E S

AMERICAN EAGLE

This is not a co-ed game. Guys and gals should play separately. All guys line up on a line. They choose one who stands thirty feet or so away (in the middle of a field). When the whistle is blown, players start running toward the guy in the middle of the field. That guy tackles one (or more if he can), and has to hold him down and say "American Eagle" three times. The rest of the players now are on the other side of the field, and now must run through two guys to get back to the original side again. This keeps up until everyone has been tackled and is in the middle of the field, and there are no more guys to run across. Give a prize to whoever lasts the longest.

ANATOMY SHUFFLE

The group pairs off by twos, and forms two circles, one inside the other. One member of each couple is on the inside circle, the other is on the outside circle.

The outer circle begins traveling in one direction (clockwise), and the inner circle goes in the opposite direction (counter-clockwise). The leader blows a whistle and yells out something like "Hand, Ear!" On this signal, the inner circle group must find their partners and place their hand on their partner's ear. Last couple to do so is out of the game. The leader calls out all sorts of combinations as the game progresses, such as:

Finger, Foot
Thigh, Thigh
Elbow, Nose
Nose, Shoulder
Head, Stomach
Etc.

The first thing called is always the inner group's part of the body, and they must find their partners, who stand in one position (they cannot move after the whistle blows) and touch their part of the body to the second item called on the partner. The last couple to remain in the game wins.

BALLOON BASKETBALL

Arrange chairs in the following manner:

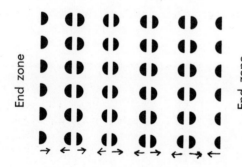

For fewer people, use fewer chairs, set up in the same way.

The rows on the ends must face inward. A round balloon is thrown into play in the two center rows and **without standing** up, the two teams try to bat the balloon with their hands into the end zone over the heads of the last row of people. If the ball (balloon) goes out of bounds, the referee tosses it back in where it went out. Five minute periods.

44

BALLOON SMASH

Each person ties a balloon (blown up) around his waist so that the balloon hangs behind him. Each person also receives a rolled-up newspaper. The object is to break everyone else's balloon and keep your own from being broken. Newspapers are the only weapon allowed. Last surviving balloon wins.

BALLOON STOMP

Each person ties a balloon (blown up) around his ankle. The object is to break everyone else's by stomping on it and to protect your own. Last person with balloon intact wins.

BARNYARD MIXER

Give each person a folded piece of paper with the name of an animal written on it. The person is not to say a word or look at the paper. He is to sit down and wait for further instruction. (To insure equal teams assign the same team every sixth person). After everyone is in and seated, the group is told to look at their team name and when the lights are turned out they are to immediately stand up and make the sound of their team only:

1. dog
2. cat
3. pig
4. duck
5. chicken
6. rooster

As soon as they find person making the same noise, they lock arms and seek the rest of the team. As soon as all of the team is together, they are to sit down. First team to find all members and sit down wins.

BIRDIE ON THE PERCH

Have couples (at least ten) form two circles—boys on the outside, girls on inside.

When whistle blows, boys' circle begins going clockwise—girls', counter-clockwise. When whistle blows again, girls are to run to their mate (who crouches down with one knee on ground) and jump up on his knee with her arms around his neck. Last couple to have the "birdie on the perch" is eliminated. Game continues until only one couple remains.

BROOM HOCKEY

This game can be played with as many as thirty or as few as five per team, but only five or six are actually on the field at one time from each team. Two teams compete by (at a whistle) running out onto the field, grabbing their brooms and swatting a volleyball placed in the center through the opposite goal. Each team has a "goalie," as in ice-hockey or soccer, who can grab the ball with his hands and throw it back out onto the playing field. If the ball goes out of bounds, referee throws it back in. The ball cannot be touched with hands, or kicked; but only hit with the broom. Score one point for each time ball passes between goal markers.

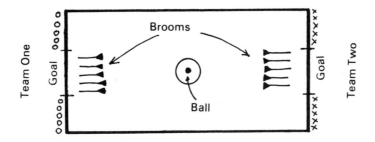

For a team with thirty members, for example, have them number off by sixes, which would give you six teams of five members each. Let all the "ones" play a three minute period, then the "two's," etc.

BLACK MAGIC

This is a "mind reading" game which always works well.

While mind reader is out of the room, the audience picks any object. The mind reader returns and the leader points to many different objects, and when he points to the chosen one, it is correctly identified by the mind reader. CODE: The chosen object is pointed to immediately **after** an object that is black has been pointed to.

BUZZ

Kids sit in a circle of some kind, and begin counting around the circle (1, 2, 3, 4, 5, etc., up to 100). Whenever a kid comes to a number containing a "7" or a multiple of "7," he says "buzz" instead of that number. For example, it would go: 1, 2, 3, 4, 5, 6, buzz, 8, 9, 10, 11, 12, 13, buzz, 15, 16, buzz, 18, 19, 20, buzz, 22, etc. If you make a mistake you go to the end of the line, or the last chair in the circle, etc., and everyone picks up where the last guy left off.

FIZZ

Fizz is the same as Buzz, only the number is "5" instead of "7."

FIZZ-BUZZ

This is obviously a combination of both games Fizz and Buzz. Going around the circle, it would sound something like this: 1, 2, 3, 4, fizz, 6, buzz, 8, 9, fizz, 11, 12, 13, buzz, fizz, 16, buzz, etc.

BUMPER BOX RELAY

Boy from each team is covered with a refrigerator box. When the signal is given, each boy is to run to the opposite wall—touch it with the box and turn back. He cannot lift the box. Hilarious results occur because none of the contestants can tell where they are going. Then have girls race in TV boxes the same way.

CATERPILLAR RELAY

For this game you need a couple of sleeping bags. One at a time, each person on a team gets into the sleeping bag (head first) and tries to reach a certain point and return. Obstacles may be placed in the way to make the game a little tougher.

COMPARISON SCAVENGER HUNT

This is a good game for camps and outdoor activities. Instead of having a "normal" scavenger hunt, where everyone goes out and brings back specific items on a list, have groups go out and bring back things like:

1. The biggest piece of wood they can find
2. The oldest nickel
3. The smelliest sock
4. The heaviest rock
5. The most worn-out shoe (or tire)
6. The rustiest tin can
7. The ugliest picture
8. The biggest leaf
9. The largest book

Have the kids bring back all the stuff and then have them one at a time bring each item up for comparison. The group with the "biggest," "oldest," etc., on each item gets points awarded for each item. Arrange for a panel of "judges" who inspect each item and choose the winners.

"DO IT ON PAPER" SHUFFLE

This is a relay game in which each person is given two pieces of paper (newspaper works fine) and they go between two points stepping only on paper. They step on the paper in front of them, then turn around and pick up the one behind them, and place it in front of them, step on it, and turn around and pick up the paper behind them, put it in front of them, step on it, and so on.

EXCEDRIN WAMP

Have each boy (4 to 6 — or as many as 100 to 300) put a paper bag loosely over his head down to his ears. Each boy has a rolled newspaper. The object is to knock the other guy's hat off without losing one's own. No one is allowed to hold his hat on.

FLAMINGO FOOTBALL

This game is really a riot, as it is actually co-ed tackle football. The only catch is, all the guys have to run, hike, pass, tackle, and everything else while holding one foot up off the ground with one hand. The results are really exciting, as the girls usually clobber the guys.

50

GROUPERS

This game can be used for as many as 1,000. Everyone crowds to the center with their arms at their sides. They are instructed to keep moving, but crowd toward the center. They must keep their arms at their sides. The leader blows a whistle or fog horn to stop all movement, and immediately yells out a number. If the number is "four," for instance, everyone must get into groups of four, lock arms, and sit down. Leaders then eliminate all those not in groups of four. This process is repeated, with different numbers each time, until all have been eliminated.

JOHN - JOHN

This can be used for groups up to 500. Form a circle using everyone. Selected leaders start the game by running to a person of opposite sex and

yelling, "What's your name?" The person replies, "Linda." The leader looks behind himself and yells, "Linda - Linda . . . Linda - Linda - Linda" while doing a little dance similar to Mexican Hat Dance. The person (Linda in this case) falls in behind the leader, putting her hands on his waist, and together they run to the opposite side of the circle. This time they both do the above together. After they finish the little dance, Linda makes an about face. The leader does the same and grabs on to Linda's waist. The new person grabs on to the previous leader's waist. Now all three proceed to the opposite side of the circle with Linda leading. She would go to a boy. Each chain continues to get longer until everyone is chosen. There would be many chains and the object would be to keep from getting hit by the other chains.

MAD-ADS

Each team receives a magazine (same one for all teams) and appoints a runner. The leader, standing in the center equidistant from each team, calls out the name of an ad which is in the magazine. Each team finds the ad in their magazine, gives it to the "runner" and the first runner to deliver the ad to the leader wins a point for his team. It is a good idea for each team to tear out all the pages of the magazine and give a few pages to each team member.

NOSE BALANCE

The participants sit on chairs facing the audience. They are to lean their heads back. A penny is placed on their nose. The object is to wiggle the penny off their noses **without moving their heads.** First to knock penny off wins. Losers get penalty.

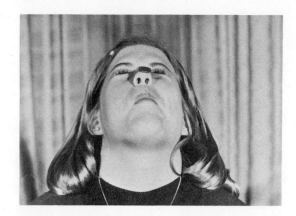

PACKS

Object is to see how many people can be stuffed into a:

Bathtub	Hula-Hoop
Hearse	Volkswagen
Coffin	Phone Booth
Ladder	Locker
Door	Tractor Tire

RHYTHM (Concentration)

Everyone in the room numbers off in a circle (1, 2, 3, 4, etc.) with the #1 guy in the end chair. The "rhythm" is begun by the #1 guy and everyone joins in by first slapping thighs, clapping hands, then snapping right hand fingers, then snapping left hand fingers in a continuous 1-2-3-4-1-2-3-4-1-2-3-4, etc., motion at a moderately slow speed. (It may speed up after everyone learns how to play.) The real action begins when the #1 guy, on the first snap of the fingers, calls out his own number, and on the second snap of the fingers, calls out somebody else's number. For example, it might sound something like this: (slap) (clap) "ONE, SIX!" and then the number six guy (as an example) might go: (slap) (clap) "SIX, TEN!" and then the number ten guy would do the same thing, calling out someone else's number on the second finger snap, and so on. If anyone misses, they go to the end of the numbered progression, and everyone who was after him before moves up one number. The object is eventually to arrive at the number one chair.

SNOWFIGHT

Two teams are separated by a row of chairs and given a six-foot stack of newspaper. They are then given one minute to wad the paper up. When the signal is given **only,** each team attempts to throw the most paper on the other team's side by the time limit. Each round (usually about 4 rounds per night) is separated by a 30-second break to find everyone who might be buried in the mountain of paper. Team with most paper on their side loses; however, there is always such a mess that a tie is declared. **Caution:** The only way to stop the throwing between rounds is to give the last person who throws something a good penalty (pie in the face, electric chair, etc.).

TOILET PAPER RELAY

Have each team line up single file and unwind roll of TP over their heads when the signal is given. Each team continues to unwind the roll up and down the line until it is gone. First team to use up the entire roll wins.

WATER BALLOON BLITZ

Divide into two teams. Give each team fifteen minutes to fill balloons (make sure there are plenty of water outlets). When the starting signal is given, everyone unloads balloons until stock is finished. Winner is the driest team. Be sure to announce the meeting before, that any participant can wear any protective items he wants (garbage can tops, goggles, etc.). Suggested number of water balloons to give out:

One team of   50 kids . . . . .200 balloons
One team of 100 kids . . . . .400 balloons
One team of 150 kids . . . . .600 balloons
One team of 200 kids . . . . .800 balloons

Be sure to use Quality #7 balloons which can be purchased at any display company or toy store.

WATER BALLOON RELAY

Use as many couples as you want. Each couple races between two points holding a water balloon between their foreheads. Of course, the couples are facing each other and walk sideways. They cannot use their hands to hold the balloon. If the balloon drops, the couple picks it up and keeps going. If it breaks, they are out of the game.

WATER BALLOON SHOT PUT

A simple game to see who can "shot put" a water balloon the farthest. To give the game added incentive, the youth leader may stand at a place "just out of reach" of the shot-putters, and they use him as a target.

WATER BALLOON TOSS

Couples line up facing each other, and are given a water balloon which they toss back and forth at a signal of some sort. Each time they move one step farther apart. Last couple to keep their water balloon in one piece wins.

WELLS FARGO

Divide the group in half. One side is the cowboys, the other side is the Indians. Mark off an eight-by-eight-foot square in the middle of the field which becomes the "bank." You will need from four to six "bags of gold" (bags of rocks will do). These should weigh about ten to fifteen pounds each. You will also need one band-aid for each player. These are stuck on everyone's forehead and become that person's "scalp." It is best to get two different colors of band-aids to distinguish the cowboys from the Indians, but you can simply mark the band-aids with X's or O's to tell them apart.

To start the game, the cowboys get the gold and have ten minutes to hide out in the woods or wherever, and at a signal, the Indians are released to try and catch them. There are two objectives to the game: (1) To get the gold (or for the cowboys to get the gold into the bank); and (2) to get scalps (band-aids). The cowboys try to get the gold in the bank, or they don't get credit for it. If the Indians can capture it (by overpowering the cowboys who have it) it is theirs and the cowboys cannot take it back. Once a cowboy is "scalped" he cannot carry the gold. Cowboys may also scalp Indians. Once anyone is scalped, he is out of the game, and must go to "boot hill."

The bags of gold are worth ten points each. (Cowboys must get it in the bank, or no points if they still have it at the end of the game.) The Indians don't have to get it in the bank to collect their points. The scalps are worth one point each. At the end of the time period (thirty minutes), team with the most points wins.

3. SPECIAL EVENTS

3. SPECIAL EVENTS

CRAZY DAZE

Decorate a bus (school bus, church bus, etc.) with poster paint, flowers, slogans, etc., or have kids decorate their cars in the same way. The wilder the better. Then, on a Saturday or a holiday, travel through a day of unusual small activities, none of which would be enough for an activity by itself. Examples might be to go to the Museum, a giant slide, games in the park, on a boat ride, various free tourist attractions, etc. The more short activities, the better. Have the kids decorate the bus or cars the night before, or begin early in the morning.

THE BLOW OUT

The theme is cars, and more specifically, tires. Select teams named after tire brands, such as Tiger Paws, Uniroyals, Firestones, etc.

DEFLATE, PATCH, PUMP UP RELAY—for fastest time.

INNER TUBE PACK

See how many kids you can get inside of a big tractor tire.

SCAVENGER HUNT

Have kids go around the neighborhood asking for old tires.

TIRE ROLL

Roll tires with a person inside—a relay game.

DIVE THROUGH

See how many kids can go through an inner tube within a specified time limit.

TIRE STACK

See which team can stack a pile of tires the highest.

TIRE SLALOM

A relay, racing tires (rolling them) through a slalom (rally) course.

TIRE EAT

Race to see which guy can eat an angel food cake the fastest (these have a hole in the middle and resemble tires) or you may do the same thing with donuts.

CAPTURE THE TUBE

Put all the tires and tubes in the middle, and have all the teams get in their corners, and at a signal, they run in and try to grab as many tires as they can, and get them back to their corner.

COME AS YOU WERE PARTY

The theme in this event is babies. Everyone is supposed to come to the party dressed up like a baby.

BEST BABY COSTUME

Judge for the funniest, most authentic, lousiest, etc.

BABY PICTURE GUESS

Everyone brings his baby picture, and you guess to see if he is recognizable.

BURPING CONTEST

Give guys a coke, they drink it, and try to see who can belch the loudest while a girl slaps them on the back.

BABY BUGGY RACE

Put a girl in a baby buggy, and have guys race them for time.

BOTTLE DRINKING CONTEST

Give several guys a baby bottle full of warm milk. See who can drink it all the fastest.

BABY FEEDING CONTEST

Have kids (guys) sit and be fed baby food by some girls to see who can finish a jar of it the fastest.

CRYING CONTEST
   See who can cry the loudest, most convincingly, etc.

MUSIC
   Sing some songs like "You must have been a beautiful baby," etc.

FIGHT NIGHTS

   Have kids come in their grubbies, meet in a vacant lot or a big backyard that can be messed up real good. Rope off a square arena—about 20 by 20 feet—and explain that all fighting will be done inside that square. Choose two boys' teams and two girls' teams of from five to ten on a team. Boys' teams fight each other first, then the girls. Spectators judge to determine the winners.
   The events are done in rounds. The teams get in their corners (like a boxing match) and the ammo is placed in the center of the arena. When the horn or whistle sounds, they come out of the corners, grab the ammo, and start fighting until the horn blows again, which ends that round.

Round One............Water Balloons
Round Two.................Tomatoes
Round Three...................Eggs
Round Four....................Flour
Round Five....................Mud

After the whole thing is over, let kids have a water fight with a hose to clean themselves off. Make sure that you have plenty of supervision, to keep kids from starting their own little fights outside of the arena.

GIRLS VS BOYS PIE CONTEST

   This is a two-week attendance contest — boys against the girls (teams do not have to be equal). Sex with most in attendance is eligible to let every person on team **who brought someone new** throw a pie in the face of anyone on the opposite team. Pies should be thrown after the meeting. Be sure to have plenty of wet towels for people to clean up.

61

OLD-TIMEY NIGHT

Each kid comes to the meeting dressed in an old-fashioned outfit of some kind (preferably 1890-ish). Award prizes for best-dressed, most authentic, etc. Prizes should be old, also, such as an 1890 Sears Catalogue, an "A-oo-gah" horn from a Model-T car, etc. Show old-time movies (W. C. Fields, Charlie Chaplin), and then perhaps after the meeting go to an ice-cream parlor, or something similar.

WEDNESDAY NIGHT AT THE MOVIES

The day in the title may be changed to match any day of the week you decide to hold this event. All the kids in your group are urged to bring old home movies (sports, baby, family, cartoons, etc.). Line up projectors (three or more) and sheets or screens. The idea is to have several films going at once on different walls or side by side on a long wall, allowing kids to mingle around and view the film they like. This creates an "art-film" atmosphere. Set up a popcorn stand, coke machine, etc. The results are fantastic.

POSTER CONTEST

Choose up teams, and each team gets a stack of magazines, magic markers, poster paints, poster board, rubber cement, etc., and from these materials, each team is to make posters describing some special event. Winning posters are chosen for originality, humor, etc., and appropriate prizes are awarded. This is a good way to get kids involved in the advertising of your program.

4. SKITS

4. SKITS

CROP DUSTER

Interviewer:

Today it is our privilege to have with us one of the men who made America great. Risking life and limb daily, he pursues his dangerous task with the calm and cool nerve of a man who is truly one of the great adventurers of modern times. His is the skill that has contributed so much to the wealth and beauty of our country and the abundance of our harvest. A real warm hand for one of California's foremost crop dusters — Dusty Crashalot!

(Enter Dusty, throwing flour from a paper bag)

Int.: Well, it's really great to have you with us today, Dusty. Just how long have you been a cropduster?

Dusty: Well, let's see now . . . mmm . . . ah . . . two weeks. Yeah, that's right. Two weeks!

Int.: Two weeks? Well, that's not a very long time.

Dusty: Well, a cropduster's life expectancy isn't very long either. We can only get one kind of insurance you know.

Int.: Oh! You **can** get insurance? I thought your job was so dangerous that you couldn't get insurance.

Dusty: Oh, yes. I'm fully covered for childbirth.

Int.: I see. Dusty, were you ever a commercial pilot before you became a cropduster?

Dusty: Oh, yes. I was pilot on a cattle ranch.

Int.: A cattle ranch? What does a pilot on a cattle ranch do?

Dusty: Oh, I just pilot here, pilot there, just piling it wherever I can pilot. (Makes like a shovel.)

Int.: Well, I meant, didn't you ever fly an airplane?

Dusty: (Pulls paper airplane from pocket) Oh, yes, why I flew one all the way from the back of the room to the blackboard once.

Int.: No, I mean while you dust crops. Don't you fly an airplane while you dust crops?

Dusty: Oh, no, that would be too dangerous. You have to have your hands free to dip in the sack!

Int.: I see . . . but . . .

Dusty: Well, I guess you could fly the plane with your feet, but you sure can't dip in the sack with your feet!

Int.: What kind of equipment do you use in your work, Dusty?

Dusty: Well, usually a whisk broom, or a feather-duster. I just walk up and down the rows dusting off the plants. They have to breathe, you know!

Int.: You actually dust the crops with a feather-duster?

Dusty: Well, once I used one of my wife's wigs. But she blew her top over that!

Int.: What is the main crop that you dust, Dusty?

Dusty: Well, let's see . . . that would be the Potunge!

Int.: What is a potunge?

Dusty: Well, it's a cross between a potato and a sponge.

Int.: Sounds interesting. Does it taste good?

Dusty: No, it tastes terrible, but, man, it sure soaks up the gravy!

Int.: Dusty, do you ever work in cotton?

Dusty: No, most of my underclothes are Japanese silk!

Int.: Dusty, tell us about your most exciting experience as a crop duster.

Dusty: Well, that would be when I was so high in my plane, that the field below looked like a postage stamp. I sent my plane into a power dive and crashed to earth.

Int.: Did you hit the field?

Dusty: What field? It **was** a postage stamp!

Int.: Have you ever had any other experiences like that, Dusty?

Dusty: Well, that would be the time when my plane lost its power at 10,000 feet.

Int.: Really? That's bad!

Dusty: Not too bad. I had my chute on.

Int.: That's good.

Dusty: Not too good. It wouldn't open.

Int.: Oooooh . . . that's bad!

Dusty: Not too bad. I headed straight for a haystack.

Int.: Well, that's good.

Dusty: No, that was bad! There was a pitchfork in the haystack.
Int.: Oh, that is bad.
Dusty: Not too bad . . . I missed the pitchfork.
Int.: That's good.
Dusty: No, that's bad. I missed the haystack too!

LAUGH IN #1

Each new line marked (—) is for a different person.
—Show me King Tut eating crackers, and I'll show you a crummy mummy!
—What would I have to give you for one little kiss?
—Chloroform!
—It's all around me! It's all around me! It's all around me! ! ! !
—What is?
—My belt.
—And now for the weather report. . . . Tomorrow muggy, followed by Tuggy, Wenggy, Thurggy and Friggy.
—Show me a fur coat that fell in the sewer, and I'll show you a stinky minky!
—I've been using embalming fluid in my car, and my motor keeps dying!
—(member of the group) co-starred with the Lone Ranger. . . . Silver was sick.
—(member of the group) went to a mind reader yesterday and was only charged half price!
—Show me a dirty bathtub, and I'll show you a grubby tubby.
—It's running down my back! It's running down my back! ! ! ! !
—What is?
—My spine.
—What do you feed a 500-pound canary?
—Anything he wants!
—Did you know that (member of the group) is a flower child?
—Yeah, he's a blooming idiot!
—Show me a tadpole caught in a rainstorm, and I'll show you a soggy froggy.
—I can't see! I can't see! I can't see! ! ! !
—Why not?
—My eyes are closed.
—Show me a bull dressed in rags, and I'll show you a bum steer.

—When I look at **roast turkey,** I want a drumstick . . . but when I look at you I want a neck!

—Does your mother mind an idiot around the house?

—No . . . drop by any time you want.

—I met my girlfriend in English class.

—Yeah, but she was so fat she sat in the first two rows.

LAUGH IN #2

—My girlfriend weighs 500 pounds . . . she isn't fat . . . but boy is she ever tall!

—I just got back from the beauty parlor.

—What was the matter . . . was it closed?

—I'm a friend of yours . . . remember me? ? ?

—Wellll . . . I can't place the name, but the breath is familiar!

—It's all over the building! It's all over the building! It's all over the building!!!

—What is?

—The roof.

—(sing) You load sixteen tons, and what do you get . . .

—A hernia!

—My hearse broke down today . . .

—Really? What happened?

—Oh, it blew a casket.

—My girl friend has a huge lower lip. But I don't mind. Her upper lip covers it.

—If I had a nickel for every girl I'd kissed . . .

—You'd be able to buy a pack of gum.

—You are going to drive me out of my mind! ! !

—That's not a drive . . . that's a putt!

—I just lost ten pounds.

—Turn around, I think I found them.

—You are just two steps ahead of an idiot!

—Well, why don't you walk. faster?

—It was only the other day I said to the lady with the wooden leg . . . PEG? . . .

LAUGH IN #3

—Will the owner of the green Ford with license number LEXBGWYURKOP-3875004 please move your car . . . your license plate is blocking the driveway.

—What do you call a German hippy?

—A flower kraut.

—Tonight's laugh-in is brought to you by Rice Krinkels . . . The cereal with 40% iron, 36% zinc, 34% phosphorous, 8% copper, and 2% steel. It doesn't snap, crackle or pop. It just lies there in the bowl and rusts.

—(member of the group) is so skinny that he has to run around in the shower to get wet!

—Latest clinical tests prove . . . that seven out of ten doctors . . .

—Leaves three!

—Show me a pineapple playing a trumpet, and I'll show you a tutti frutti.

—The hardest assignment I ever had was in Biology. I had to write an essay on the belly of a frog. The only trouble was, I couldn't get the frog in the typewriter!

—(member of the group) is so skinny that his striped pajamas only have one stripe.

—(member of the group) is so skinny that when he sticks his tongue out and stands sideways, he looks like a zipper!

—Confucius once say . . . A bird in the hand . . . sure makes it hard to blow your nose.

—Did you hear about my new invention . . . the square bathtub?

—No . . . what good is a square bathtub?

—It eliminates the ring.

—Well, I just invented an electric car, and drove it all the way from Chicago to Los Angeles on only twelve cents worth of electricity.

—Really? Why that's fantastic!

—Yeah, but it cost me 53,000 dollars for extension cords.

—(member of the group) is so skinny that he has to wear skis in the shower to keep from going down the drain! ! !

—Confucius once say . . . always cross the street with the light. That is, if you can rip it out of the pavement.

LETTER FROM CAMP

(A great camp gag. Announce that this letter was intercepted at the Post Office. Include appropriate names, etc.)

Dear _____,

My week at camp is just about over. _____ is a nice place to camp—30,000,000 mosquitos can't be wrong. They told us that every room overlooked a beautiful canyon. They also overlooked inside toilets, mattresses and running water. My room is so small, the mice are hunchbacked. It does have a nice bath. . . . I'd rather have a bed.

The cabin is modern — it has chrome doorknobs, chrome banisters, chrome windowsills—as a matter of fact, it's the chromiest room I've ever been in. They have an Indian Village here. An old chief lives there and his name is Chief Running Water. He has three sons, Hot, Cold, and Luke. When I visited there, Luke wasn't feeling so hot.

Really, this is the place for mosquitoes. It's getting so you don't want to swat any of them because you don't want to kill your own flesh and blood. We got up early and went water skiing on the lake this morning. First time I ever went. I got behind that boat, on the skis, line in my hand—then one ski went one way, the other went the other way and **laugh.** . . . I thought I'd split! While I was recuperating the camp nurse, Heather, told me to drink a glass of warm milk after a hot bath. Dumb nurse, I couldn't even finish drinking the hot bath.

Love,

MELODRAMA — AN EVENING WITH GRANDMA

This play requires absolutely **no** acting ability, and is a guaranteed winner at camps, rallies, and youth meetings of all kinds.

THE CHARACTERS (not counting narrator)

1. Manuel—dressed in black
2. Maggie—the fair maiden
3. Patrick—dressed in white
4. Zingerella—the housekeeper
5. and 6.   The Curtains
7. and 8.   Hours
9.   The Sun
10.   Night

PROPS NEEDED

1. Pitcher of water
2. Podium
3. Chalk
4. Trading or postage stamps
5. Broom
6. Pail
7. Banana
8. Police whistle
9. Iron
10. Rope
11. Two salt shakers
12. Large wooden match
13. Notes
14. Signs
    a. Curtains—2
    b. Stairs

c. Time
d. "No" (written on small pieces of paper)
   —about 30 or more
e. Hours—2
f. Sun
g. Night

THE NARRATOR READS THE FOLLOWING SCRIPT (Actors pantomime the action as described in the **footnotes** section below)

The curtains part.[1]

The sun rises.[2]

Our play begins.

Manuel de Populo, son of a wealthy merchant, is in his study, carefully poring over his notes.[3] He stamps his feet[4] impatiently, and calls for his maid, Zingerella.

Zingerella tears down the stairs[5] and trips into the room.[6] "Go fetch Maggie O'Toole," demands Manuel. Zingerella flies[7] to do her master's bidding.

Time passes.[8]

Manuel crosses the floor—once—twice—thrice.[9] At last Maggie comes sweeping into the room.[10]

"For the last time, will you marry me?" insists Manuel. Maggie turns a little pale.[11]

"**No**," she shouts. "A thousand times **No**." [12]

"Then I will have to cast you into the dungeon," says Manuel, in a rage.

She throws herself at his feet.[13] "Oh, Sir," she pleads, "I appeal to you."[14]

Haughtily he says, "Your appeal is fruitless." [15] At that, Manuel stomps out of the room.[16]

Maggie flies about in a dither.[17] Oh, if only Patrick would come, he would save her!

The hours pass slowly.[18] Finally Maggie takes her stand,[19] and scans[20] the horizon. Suddenly she hears a whistle.[21] Could it be . . . ?

"Maggie, it is I, my love, your Patrick! ! !"

He enters the room and tenderly presses her hand.[22] She throws him a line.[23] Just at that moment, Manuel re-enters and challenges Patrick to a duel. In a fury, they assault each other.[24] Finally Manuel gives up the match,[25] and departs. "At last, you are mine!" says Patrick. He leads his love away into the night.[26] The sun sets.[27] Night falls.[28] The curtains come together[29] and our play is ended.

FOOTNOTES

1. Two people with signs that say "curtains" walk away from each other beginning at center of the stage.
2. Person with "sun" sign, stands up.
3. He pours water from a pitcher all over some notes.
4. Licks stamps, sticks on shoes.
5. Rips down a sign that says "stairs" and tears it up.
6. Falls down (trips).
7. Waves arms in flying motion.
8. Guy holding "time" sign walks across stage.
9. Takes chalk and makes three big "X's" on the floor.
10. Sweeps with a broom.
11. Turns a pail upside down.
12. Throws paper with "no" on them.
13. Falls at his feet and lies there.
14. Hands him a banana peel.
15. Hands the banana peel back.
16. Stomps his feet.
17. Waves arms in flying manner.
18. Two people with "hours" signs walk across the stage.
19. Stands behind podium.
20. Hand above eyes in searching motion.
21. Patrick blows police whistle.
22. Takes iron and irons her hand.
23. Throws a rope at him.
24. Take salt shakers and sprinkle each other.
25. Hands Patrick a wooden match.
26. Bump into the guy with the night sign.
27. Sun sits down.
28. "Night" falls down.
29. "Curtains" walk toward each other.

LEAVING HOME — Two characters

A man sits in a chair reading a newspaper. A woman enters with a coat on and carrying a suitcase. She is apparently very upset. The man in the chair could care less.

Woman: I've had it! I'm through! I'm leaving this crummy rotten house and all these crummy kids and going home to mother! I'm sick and tired of ironing, mopping and cleaning up after you day in and day out! I tell you, I've had it! No more! I'm leaving and don't ask me to come back because I am leaving for good! (sobbing) Good-by! (stomps out of the room).

Man: (somewhat bewildered, turns to an offstage room and yells) Alice, dear! The maid just quit.

5. CREATIVE COMMUNICATION

5. CREATIVE COMMUNICATION

DISCUSSIONS

The discussions can be an effective means of communication if done correctly. The following guidelines are most important:

1. The biggest hindrance to open and honest communication in the church is the lack of freedom to say that which does not fit within the confines of "correct" theology. The atmosphere of the discussion must be one of complete freedom to say what one believes regardless of its adherence to what others believe. Therefore, the leader should only be concerned with keeping order rather than guiding the group to the correct answer(s).

2. Establish simple ground rules. The important thing to realize is that attitude plays a significant role. The rules should be given in a humorous way and the leader should go overboard to assure the group that there will be no penalty for honesty and frankness. Possible ground rules might simply be: 1) Don't talk while someone else is talking; 2) Wait until the person is done speaking before you react.

3. Always maintain an attitude of objectivity as a leader. Refrain from giving away your opinion by the way you react or the way you ask a question.

4. Questions should be well thought out so that they are as objective as possible. Avoid "loaded" questions. (Example: Do non-Christians enjoy life or do they just **think** they do?)

The following discussion topics and questions are meant only as guidelines. Certainly you will adapt them to fit your own needs.

CHEATING

1. Describe some of the ways kids cheat in school.
2. Why do kids cheat?
3. Is cheating always wrong, if at all?

CHURCH

1. What don't you like about church? What do you like?
2. Is the church relevant?
3. What is or should be the purpose of the church?

CLIQUES

1. What is a clique?
2. Are cliques wrong? Why or why not?

PARENTS

1. What bugs you most about your parents?
2. What do you like most about your parents?
3. Would you like to follow your parents' example? Why or why not?

PHONIES

1. Think of a person you consider a phony. Describe him or her (don't use names).
2. What is the worst kind of phony?
3. Aren't we all phonies in one sense or another?

PRINCIPAL OF THE UNIVERSE

1. If you could be principal of your school, what would you do?
2. If you could be President what would you do?
3. If you could be principal of the universe (God), what would you do?

RACISM

1. Are all whites racists?
2. Does Christianity make any difference when it comes to the racial issue?
3. Should whites help the black community or should whites just help the white community?

ROCK MUSIC

1. What are the most common gripes you hear from adults about "your" music? Are they right?
2. What is good about rock music, if anything?
3. What is bad about rock music, if anything?

SEX

1. How far is too far?
2. What is the purpose of sex?
3. Can a Christian be completely uninhibited when it comes to sex?

SWEARING

1. What is swearing?
2. What about "borderline words" or "minced oaths" like "darn"?
3. Is swearing wrong?

SUICIDE

1. Think of a creative new way to commit suicide.
2. Tell us about an experience you have had with suicide (a friend, etc.).
3. Is suicide wrong?
4. If you only had a few minutes to talk someone out of suicide what would you say?

VIOLENCE

1. Is violence ever justified?
2. What issues, if any, would you consider important enough to merit violence?
3. Can violence ever be stopped?

DRINKING

1. Now that drugs are "in" is drinking "out"?
2. Is all drinking wrong?
3. Did Jesus drink? Does it make any difference whether He did or not?

COP-OUT

Invite a policeman to answer questions from the group. Have each person write out a question on blank paper. (Be sure to tell them **not** to put their name on the paper.) The policeman then reads them back and answers them and discusses the answers with the group. Be sure to set a time limit for each answer like two minutes (not including discussion).

DRUGS

If you haven't discussed this yet . . . forget it!

FREEDOM

1. Is it possible to be completely free?
2. What limits freedom?
3. Define freedom.

GOD

1. What is your concept of God?
2. Does it matter what you call God?
3. What difference, if any, does a belief in God make?

HELL

1. Do you believe in hell? Why or why not?
2. What is your concept of hell?
3. Does it make any difference whether you believe in hell or not?

MODELS

Give a piece of paper to each group member and have them write the name of a person they most respect or would like to be like. Of course, don't have them include their own name. Read them all back to the group (some of them, hopefully, will be funny).

1. What are the most important characteristics of your model?
2. Does Christianity have any contemporaries you would like as a model?
3. Do your models affect your life?

WILL OF GOD

The following questions should be duplicated and given to each member of the group to answer with a "yes" or "no." Then go back and discuss them.

		YES	NO
1.	Has God ever communicated with you directly?	☐	☐
2.	Does God have an absolute moral standard for man?	☐	☐
3.	Is man responsible to God for his action?	☐	☐
4.	Can two people be led by God to do that which is the opposite of the other?	☐	☐
5.	Has God already chosen a wife or husband for you?	☐	☐
6.	If you make a wrong major decision, can you ever be in God's will?	☐	☐
7.	Have you ever consulted the Bible when making a decision and found help?	☐	☐
8.	Should God be consulted when selecting a career?	☐	☐
9.	Should God be consulted when buying your clothes?	☐	☐

THE DISCUSSION "WRAP-UP"

The "wrap-up" to the discussion is one of the most important parts. Of course, you may decide to leave the discussion "open-end" and not have any concluding statements. If, however, you use a "wrap-up" the following guidelines are important:

1. Have a general outline prepared ahead of time but be flexible enough to be able to encompass many of the statements made in the actual discussion. Use direct quotes from the discussion. A general outline could be:
   a. Light remarks about the topic spiced with a personal story or illustration.
   b. Define the issue, i.e., "Although most of our discussion has centered around whether drinking is right or wrong, it seems to me that morality is **not** the issue. In my opinion, the issue is . . ."
   c. Relationship to Christianity — "In short, what are the spiritual implications?"

2. Be sure to summarize what has been said in the discussion. Do not take issue with what was said. Simply offer your remarks as something to be considered also.

THE ISLAND AFFAIR

This is a great discussion that is entertaining as well as extremely interesting. Use the diagram below while telling story.

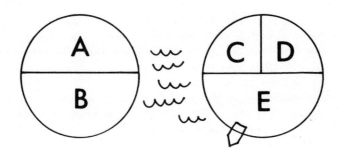

The two circles represent two islands surrounded by shark infested waters. As a result of a shipwreck only five survivors landed on the islands. A is a teenage boy who was unfortunately separated from his girlfriend C and fortunately separated from his girlfriend's mother D. B is another teenage boy not acquainted with A, and E is an older man who is kind of a loner.

The situation is this: C loves A very much and vice-versa. But there is one big problem. C can't get to A without a boat. This made C very unhappy and one day while walking around the island she discovered that E had just finished making a boat. Immediately C asks E to let her use the boat to get to A but E refuses. "After all," he reasons, "I have worked very hard and long to build this boat. My time is worth something. Give me all the money you have and I will let you use the boat!" Unfortunately, C doesn't have any money. E then offers to let C use the boat if she will make love to him. C asks for time to think and asks her mother, D, for advice. Her mother says something like this, "I understand how much you love A and I know it seems hopeless that you'll ever get to see A again, but sometimes if we do what we know is wrong to get what we want, we end up losing what we wanted. I think it would be best for you to wait and turn down E's offer. Something will come along, I'm sure."

After many days of soul-searching C decides to accept E's offer and she makes love to E. E keeps his part of the bargain and rows C to A's island. A and C are very happy and embrace and laugh and talk. After a while, C sits down with A and tells him of the hopeless situation she was in. She confesses that she made love to E but emphasizes that it was because of her deep love for A. A is deeply hurt. He tries to understand but after long discussion and thought tells C that although he loves her very much he could not continue their relationship knowing that she loved another man. C tries to change his mind but to no avail.

However, while all this was going on B was listening from behind the bushes. When A finally departs B quickly comes to C's side and tells her that he does understand why she made love to E and would be willing to accept her and love her in spite of what she did. C accepts and B and C go off together. (End of story.)

Give each kid a piece of paper and pencil and have them list the people in the story from best to worst using 1 as best and 5 as worst. Their paper would simply look like this: 1-A, 2-D, 3-E, etc. Have the papers handed in without names.

Discussion

The Girl (C)
  1. Was she justified in what she did to get to A?
  2. Should she have accepted B's proposal?

The Boy (A)
  1. Should he have accepted C anyway since she loved him so much?
  2. Was his decision right or wrong?

The Mother (D)
  1. Was her advice good or bad?

The Man (E)
  1. Was what he did right or wrong?

The Other Boy (B)
  1. Why did he accept C?

Wrap-Up

Each of these people represents a value:
  A=Morals
  B=Sex
  C=Popularity
  D=Wisdom
  E=Money

Normally, the rating most audiences give these values is as follows:
  1-D (Wisdom)
  2-A (Morals)
  3-E (Money)
  4-B (Sex)
  5-C (Popularity)

Isn't it true, however, that although intellectually Wisdom and Morality are important when we make a decision in practice we place more importance on material or external matters like sex, popularity and money. Something inside of us causes us to live contrary to our value judgments. We face much the same frustration that Paul did in Romans 7. Why?

It is very important to practice giving this story and to know it well. You may change the dialog suggested but just make sure the dialog correctly represents the value it stands for.

GROUPERS

Groupers is the name given to short "written discussions." They consist of a "complete this sentence in ten words or less" type of statement, which the audience completes and passes in. These work great as a springboard into the message of the evening, such as the grouper "Happiness is . . ." (see below). They also provide a means by which the normally quiet guy or girl can express himself (or herself) without being vocal. Usually, because of the normal percentage of wise-guys in the crowd, groupers also provide an entertaining and humorous break in the meeting as well.

The procedure for using groupers is very simple. A basic plan for their use is as follows:

1. Each person in the group receives a pencil (golf pencils work fine), and a piece of paper.
2. Tell each person to write what has been instructed on the piece of paper.
   a. Answers may be funny or serious.
   b. Be sure no one else sees it.
   c. Don't put your name on it.
   d. Fold it in half and hand it in to the leader.
3. Keep pushing them to finish quickly. If they can't think of anything to put down, they don't have to answer. There will be enough answers without theirs.
4. After all are collected, read them back, one at a time, screening those that are duplicates or are too crude. (You'll get a few of those . . .)
5. After you have read them, use an appropriate wrap-up. The best way to do this is to share how **you** would have completed the sentence. Another way is to simply agree with some that you read, and explain why. Another way to wrap up is to ask the crowd to decide which answer they liked best, and perhaps have a brief discussion on why they chose that particular answer.

For example, one grouper which is always successful is "Happiness is . . ." and the audience completes the sentence, inserting what happiness is to them. You will receive many different answers, ranging from ". . . not having to listen to our Youth Director talk!" to ". . . knowing God in a very personal way." After reading the answers back to the group, you could wrap up with an outline similar to the one below which has been used.

I. Everyone is truly looking for happiness.
   A. For example, a teenage girl wrote in to Ann Landers and said:
      Dear Ann,
      Happiness is having parents that love you.
      Happiness is being as well dressed as anyone in your crowd.
      Happiness is having your own room.
      Happiness is getting that telephone call you've been waiting for.
      Happiness is being popular.
      Happiness is having parents who don't fight.
      Happiness is something I don't have.
                                    signed,
                                    Sixteen and Un-happy.

B. Happiness is truly "different things to different people."

II. What is true happiness? What is the secret formula? Psychologists tell us that three things are needed to achieve happiness.

   A. Someone to love. (Explain the true meaning of "love.") This is not a selfish love or a "you scratch my back, I'll scratch yours" type of love relationship. It is unselfish as in First Corinthians 13.

   B. Something to do. A purpose in life that brings satisfaction. (Explain the importance of getting a good education, etc.)

   C. Something to hope for. A goal in life. (A runner in a race has got to have a goal, or there's no use in running. . . .)

III. How do we achieve these three things in our life? The easiest and most rewarding way is found in the Bible. Psalm 144:15 says: "Happy is that people whose God is the Lord." In other words, when we let God become the Lord of our lives, we achieve the three things which psychology says is important to obtain happiness.

   A. Someone to love. God gives us the supreme example of love to follow in His Son, Jesus Christ. A human love relationship controlled by God also has greater dimension than a love relationship apart from God's control.

   B. Something to do. God has given each of us talents and abilities and can channel those abilities for us.

   C. Something to hope for. "All things work together for good to them that love God . . . ; The gift of God is eternal life . . ." etc.

IV. There is no greater happiness than giving God a chance in your life.

The above outline is merely a sample of what can be done to wrap up a grouper. Below are some more suggested "groupers" which are possibilities.

1. Security is . . .
2. Misery is . . .
3. I fear most . . .
4. I wish I were . . .
5. I wish I were not . . .
6. I wish I had . . .
7. I wish I had not . . .
8. I wish I could . . .

9. Girls are . . .
10. Boys are . . .
11. Love is . . .
12. The worst thing a person could do is . . .
13. What always makes me mad is . . .
14. If I could do anything, and no one else would know, I would . . .
15. Honesty is . . .
16. I always cry when . . .
17. I always laugh when . . .
18. I hate . . .
19. If I were principal of the high school, I would . . .
20. If I had a million dollars, I would . . .
21. If my parents left me alone for a month, I would . . .
22. If I had X-ray vision I would . . .

HONESTY SURVEY

Print up the following questions on sheets of paper, pass out to the group, and give them ten minutes or so to answer, being as honest as possible. (Especially since the survey is on honesty!) This gets them really thinking about the subject in depth, and is a good preliminary to either a discussion or message on honesty.

1. Try to recall the most recent lie that you have told.
2. Try to imagine a situation where personal dishonesty would be worthwhile.
3. What is the most dishonest act a person can perform?
4. Name an incident where your friends were dishonest with you.
5. What things do you encounter that make it difficult for you to be honest?

RED-BLACK SIMULATION GAME (Discussion on Competition and Trust)

Actually this is more of a learning experience than a "game." Although a game of sorts is involved, the object is to point out the importance of **trust** in our lives, and also to help kids understand their natural tendency to compete and to win, even when "winning" is not our goal.

THE SIMULATION GAME

(1) The only props needed are about twenty 3 x 5 cards, two pencils, and some play money. Play money can be obtained from a Monopoly set, etc.

(2) Divide the group into two groups. (Avoid using the word "team" as it implies competition.) It might be a good idea for you to explain that an experiment (rather than a "game") is about to take place. The kids can number off 1, 2, 1, 2, etc., or they can just divide up any way they please.

(3) Give the following instructions: **Each group will have nine opportunities to choose a color, either red or black. The choices are worth money. Here's the way it works: If both groups choose "black," both groups will get three dollars. If both choose "red," both will lose three dollars. But if one group chooses "red," and the other group chooses "black," the "red" choice gets five dollars and the "black" choice loses five dollars.** Explain this as many times as it takes until everyone understands.

(4) After basic scoring procedure is explained, then tell the group that there are two simple requirements to fulfill:

(a) **To make as much money as you possibly can.**

(b) **To not hurt anyone.**

(5) Have the two groups go to opposite sides of the room (or preferably to two different rooms) and decide on their first color choice. You remain in the center with the money.

Note: It is important that the two groups not know what the other is doing.

(6) Each group selects a leader (in any manner they wish) who brings his group's decision to you on a 3 x 5 card which you furnish him. Written on the card should be either "red" or "black." You award money to the groups as per instructions in (3).

(7) Game continues. After the fourth attempt at color choosing, you ask if the groups wish to negotiate. The group can pick one person from the other group. After this, announce that the next choice will be worth three times as much money. (Don't announce this change in value until after the negotiating has been done, if they choose to negotiate at all.)

(8) Finish all nine rounds and then get together to discuss what took place, and who made how much money.

THE DISCUSSION

Ask the entire group's reaction to the following questions.

(a) What was your group's strategy; that is, how did you decide just what color to choose?

(b) Did your group fulfill the game requirements? How? (See No. 4 above.)

(c) Did you trust the other group?

(d) Why did (or didn't) you want to negotiate with the other group?

(e) When did you decide (after which choice) to try and beat the other group?

(f) To beat the other group, did you have to emphasize one requirement over the other?

(g) How did you treat the "minority" voice in your group?

AFTER THE DISCUSSION

It is suggested that you include the following general points in your concluding remarks or "lesson" from the simulation game:

(1) Both groups became involved in competition even though no mention of competition or of beating the other group was made. This shows man's natural tendency to satisfy his ego with being superior to others, or selfishness and greed. It is this natural tendency that in many ways causes poverty, oppression, and war in the world. Show through Scripture how Christ came to set us free from this nature. See Romans 3 - 7.

(2) Trust and cooperation were essential if both groups were going to benefit. Most human relationships today, however, lack trust or cooperation. (Give examples—politics, business, ordinary friendships.) As a result, we find it difficult to trust **God,** because we are afraid He won't keep His word, or that we are not being told the truth. But God has trusted us by making the first move—sending His Son. We have to make our choice also by "trust" or by "faith," believing that surely a decision to take God at His word when He offers us life through His Son, will result in a peaceful coexistence between man and God. (Elaborate on this—John 3:16, Romans 6:23, John 1:10, II Corinthians 5:17, etc.).

Note: The key to the success of this activity is to what degree the two groups actually compete against each other. You cannot encourage competition at all; however, there are ways to make it even more inevitable. One way is to award (instead of play money) something that is **really** worth something or something that the kids really want, such as candy, or real money (pennies or nickels, etc.).

CHRISTIANITY QUESTIONNAIRE

The following questionnaire is excellent for testing your kids' knowledge of basics in the faith. Many of the questions are deliberately antagonistic toward Christianity, but then so is the world, and kids need to have some answers. It is suggested that you give this questionnaire to your group one week, let them fill it out at home (or during the meeting if you have time) and then discuss each question the following week.

1. Why do you believe in God? Don't use the Bible as proof, because I don't believe the Bible is true.
2. If God is so loving, how can He send nonbelievers to Hell?
3. Also, if God is so loving, how come He allows so much pain and suffering to go on in the world?
4. Christians say that God is omnipotent. If this is so, could God make a rock that was too heavy for Him to pick up?
5. Christians are always talking about the power of prayer. It seems to me that it is all in their minds, and that it is nothing more than a psychological boost. Also, when prayer does come true, it is probably just a coincidence. Can you show evidence to prove otherwise?
6. Christians believe that God forgives them for their sins if they ask Him to. This seems to be just an easy way to clear one's conscience, and is used by Christians to ease their minds. Which explanation is correct?
7. Hasn't science disproved the Bible? For example, evolution clearly eliminates any possibility of Creation as it is in Genesis.
8. Considering all the technological advances which have been made recently, and the fact that scientists are about to create life in a test tube, it seems to me that God is no longer needed as an explanation for things being as they are. Why then do Christians continue to believe in God?

9. What is so special about the Bible?
10. Are the right books in the Bible? If so, how do you know?
11. Is the Bible really true, or is it just a book of myths and fairy tales which make people feel good?
12. Why is religion even necessary? Science is the only answer for educated people.
13. Who says Christians are right and all the other religions are wrong?
14. How do you know that Jesus Christ is who He said He was?
15. How can Christians believe in the Resurrection? What evidence is there to support this belief?
16. How do you know Christ is alive today?
17. Christians are always talking about love, kindness, doing for others, etc., but in reality they are all hypocrites. How can you expect anyone to want to join this kind of group?
18. What is so special about having a personal relationship with Jesus Christ? If someone wants to get "high," there is always drugs, alcohol, and sex.
19. How can you believe in the Trinity? It is impossible for three people to be one person.
20. If God created man perfectly in the beginning, how come Adam sinned?
21. Why does the church spend so much on big, fancy buildings?
22. Why does the church talk about money so much?

6. PUBLICITY AND PROMOTION